Mustard Seed
Mentality

*UnscRipted Pearls of Wisdom from
a Wife, Mother, and Entrepreneur*

DR. JADE L. RANGER

PALMETTO
PUBLISHING

Charleston, SC
www.PalmettoPublishing.com

*Mustard Seed Mentality: UnscRxipted Pearls
of Wisdom from a Wife, Mother, and Entrepreneur*

Copyright © 2021 by Dr. Jade L. Ranger

First Edition

Hardcover ISBN: 978-1-63837-984-3
Paperback ISBN: 978-1-63837-983-6
eBook ISBN: 978-1-63837-985-0

So Jesus said to them, "Because of your unbelief; for assuredly, I say to you, if you have faith as a mustard seed, you will say to this mountain, 'Move from here to there,' and it will move; and nothing will be impossible for you."

—Matthew 17:20 (NKJV)

Table of Contents

Mustard Seed Men·tal·i·ty | \ men-ˈta-lə-tē \
Definition of mustard seed mentality
Faith-based <u>mental</u> power, capacity, or outlook—having confidence that anything is possible if you trust in God and believe in yourself.

Introduction

My seven-year-old son asked me, "Mommy, why are you sad?" It was April 15, 2021. I was lying down with my children as they prepared to go to bed. I'd had a long day and an even longer week. I felt as though all of my responsibilities were weighing me down and everything that was going on in our country and the world was affecting my psyche. Holding "it" all together had always been my thing, whatever "it" was. Always prepared, organized, and ready to conquer "it" all was the impression that I gave most people, when the reality was that I could be hanging on by a thread. I know what you're probably thinking: "I was hoping to get some positivity and silver linings from this book." My intro isn't too convincing that we are heading in an uplifting direction, is it? Go ahead and insert an LOL here. Over the course of this book, I will give you some pearls of wisdom that I've learned along the way and tools on how to address your feelings head-on. I'll be transparent. I want you to get an open and honest perspective from me, not the filtered "that's too taboo" commentary that we've gotten so accustomed to.

So, as I was saying, I was lying down with my boys, Jacob (7) and Joshua (3). Josh had fallen right to sleep. Jacob, on the other hand, was somewhat alert and aware that I was choking back tears. When he asked me why I was sad, it took the little energy that I had left to respond, "Mommy is just tired." It was a simple statement but one that encompassed all of my emotions in that moment; mentally, physically, and spiritually I was burned-out. We'd basically just hit the one-year mark since a pandemic swept the world and life as we knew it. Two more unarmed, young men of color had just been killed by the police within the past week. And while business was booming at my pharmacy and I was thankful, my husband and I had just agreed that it was time to hire another associate. I was pretty much over the virtual learning and wanted to be done with having to facilitate schoolwork at home for my first grader. My workout routine had been nonexistent for almost a month, and my sleep pattern had been thrown off; I was exhausted. Ultimately, I knew that I was extremely blessed. My family was alive and well, and I had not lost anyone to COVID-19. The pandemic hadn't caused us to shut down our small business, and my children were thriving in school in spite of all of the challenges caused by the coronavirus. I'd beat myself up about why I was feeling a little down and overly anxious. Does any of this sound familiar? Of course, it does! While our lives are different and our daily struggles may vary, I don't think there's a mom out there who wasn't on the verge of a nervous breakdown at some point over this past year.

All of our usual responsibilities and tasks basically doubled overnight. We went from managing our home fronts and working (either inside or outside of our homes), to balancing working from home, virtual learning, Zoom meetings, drive-by birthday parties, and making sure that our houses were stocked with every paper product known to man. It had been a whirlwind of a year to say the least, and I felt like everything was hitting me all at once like a ton of bricks.

As I lay there reflecting on how I had gotten to this moment, the failures and triumphs, the joy and the pain, the feeling of certainty and the second-guessing, it hit me—the faith of a mustard seed had sustained me throughout my life. At some point, I developed what I like to refer to as "mustard seed mentality," and it had carried me this far. So I took a deep breath and trusted my faith to move mountains.

The Marriage Compromise

S o often when we say those magical words "I do," we think that we will live happily ever after with our Prince Charming and in a permanent state of euphoria. While I believe that can be true, the reality is that when life meets marriage, things don't always work out how we planned. When it comes to marriage, I'm by no means an expert. However, I believe that I can share some of the lessons that I've learned in my own marriage thus far over the course of the past decade. Of course, every marriage is different and different strokes will work for different folks. But ultimately I think you will find at least one of the following tips to be helpful.

➢ Communication is key!

As women we sometimes think that our significant other should just "get us" and know what we are thinking and how we feel. After all, we expressed certain feelings or thoughts in the past, right? *Wrong*! Men and women alike can fall into the trap of expecting our partners to read our minds or just sense what we are currently feeling. When we expect anyone to know how we are feeling, we are setting ourselves up as well as the other party involved. What usually follows are unmet expectations and feelings of disappointment on our part and feelings of frustration or inadequacy for our better half. Why not skip the drama of speculation and decide to just be straightforward with our spouses? When we have open communication, it can save us a lot of back and forth and headaches in the long run. Once we realize the power of communication, we often become liberated and feel more comfortable being open and honest about how we feel. Don't get discouraged if your honesty is initially met with a little bit of pushback; keep it going so that both you and your partner come to expect transparency from one another.

Now please don't twist my words; what I am _not_ saying is to go off on your spouse and curse them out. Just like with anything else in life, your approach when communicating your feelings is _everything_. Always be mindful of how you are communicating and do so with love. There are multiple ways you can deliver your message, and your tone and intention usually determine how your message is received. Obviously, if you say, "Shut up, I can't focus!" it will be received much differently than if you say, "Do you mind bringing your volume down a bit; I'm trying to focus on my briefing for my meeting tomorrow." The words you choose and how you say them matter.

Everyone who knows and loves me knows that I have a serious case of OCD. At times it's joked about and other times I can tell that I annoy people with my incessant need for cleanliness and order. It's no different with my husband. While he's thankful for a wife that cares about keeping our house clean, it took constant reminding over a couple of years early on in our marriage to get him to fully contribute to our housework consistently. At first I would kind of spaz out and go off on rants about how "I'm not a maid" and "I shouldn't be the only one cleaning up our living spaces!" Don't get me wrong, my husband has never been a slob. Even when we first started dating, his bachelor's pad was never a pigsty. I always thought, "He's not too bad for a guy" as it relates to his tidiness. I think a lot of men become complacent when it comes to household work because they get used to the women in their lives picking up after them. Whenever I would express myself to my husband, I usually did so in anger. That was my first problem; I was letting anger build up instead of addressing the issue directly when it first began to bother me.

As women we can sometimes avoid expressing ourselves because we don't want to nag our partners. We are afraid of seeming petty or nitpicking. For women of color, and Black women in particular, we don't want to appear angry or too feisty or be compared to whatever other stereotypes we are constantly bogged down by. So instead of just speaking up, we suffer in silence. This is a "lose-lose" approach all the way around. By letting our feelings fester, we then open ourselves up to feelings of resentment or contempt for our spouses; neither are good, and that scenario never plays out well for any couple. After maturing a little and gaining a bit more experience under my belt, I've learned how my husband responds to me based on how I communicate my feelings to him. We each have our own love languages and tend to be more or less receptive depending on how we perceive that our own feelings are being taken into account. I'm saying all of this to say that there is nothing wrong with communicating how you feel to your significant other. As long as you are being mindful of their feelings, being respectful, and are open to them communicating their feelings in return, you can't go wrong.

Now whenever I feel like my husband has started to slack off here and there with contributing to chores around the house, instead of playing victim and getting myself worked up, I choose to communicate my feelings in a way in which I know that he will understand and can relate to. Some will say I shouldn't have to keep saying the same thing over and over again; that's true. But the good thing is that after a while I didn't have to keep saying the same thing or address the matter as frequently. Eventually, Henry became accustomed to my expectations of him because I clearly communicated them to him.

I didn't expect him to guess what I wanted him to do; I spelled it out for him so that there would be no confusion. Instead of expecting him to do everything that I would normally do on my days off of work, I started leaving him directions. He appreciated having a honey-do list that laid out exactly what needed to be done, and I enjoyed coming home to tasks being completed and things being squared away around our house. That's what I call a win-win for everyone!

Communication isn't only key in romantic relationships or relationships in general but also with ourselves. Yes, it's important to have open communication in order to create healthy relationships, but it's equally, if not more, important to be honest with ourselves. This is a concept that took me quite a while to learn and even longer to actually put into practice. If I'm not honest with myself about my own desires and what's truly important to me, then how can I clearly communicate my expectations to others? So just like with anything else in life, in order to become a great communicator, you have to start with the person staring back at you in the mirror. I suggest taking an inner poll and writing down things that are a deal breaker when it comes to relationships and areas where you're willing to compromise. I mentioned before that I have a tendency to be a bit OCD (OK, you got me…more than just a tendency), so you know I love a good list (of any kind really). Once you know how you want your relationship to look, take steps to put your preferences into action. This is a good exercise for individuals and couples alike.

Something that I personally struggled with was my innate desire for things in my marriage to be fifty-fifty. Growing up, my father groomed my sister and me to be confident, assertive, and most importantly independent. As a child, I saw my father wash dishes and aid in keeping our house clean. Looking back, I now realize that it was my childish perception that interpreted those observations to mean that in marriage the husband and wife split the household duties up half-and-half. Now that I am a wife, I realize that in actuality things play out very differently.

I believe my husband goes above and beyond to help me manage our household. Regardless, as women we know that no matter how helpful our husbands/significant others may be, we will always carry the brunt of the work. Women wear so many hats simultaneously, including but not limited to wife, mother, working woman, chef, housekeeper, taxi driver, event planner, nurse, personal shopper, keeper of the family calendar, PTA volunteer, personal cheerleader, and the list goes on and on; and that doesn't even include our social lives. Many of us are involved in church, community service, sororities, social clubs, and so much more.

Men tend to be bigger picture type of individuals (more on this later)—meaning, they are pleased when things at home are taken care of, but they may not fully appreciate or understand all of the effort that we as women put into keeping up with everything all at once.

For years (and even now at times) I prayed that God would give me the heart of Mary versus the attitude of Martha (Luke 10:38–42 NIV). I then had to be honest with myself and admit that oftentimes I put more on myself than I need to. Don't get me wrong; my plate is legitimately full. However, I tend to put unnecessary pressure on myself, which results in unwanted stress. My constant need to strive for perfection in every area of my life was not only physically, mentally, and emotionally draining but it almost drove me crazy. I wasted way too much time trying to cram thirty-two hours' worth of work into my twenty-four-hour days (sound familiar?). Then one of my mentors gave me a very sound piece of advice I'll share with you here—the only thing that deserves 100 percent from me is God, my family, and my business; everything else may only get 60 percent of my time and attention. She told me to be strategic when deciding what deserves my time and attention and to exert my energy on things that will serve me back. I thought that was great advice and took some time to think long and hard about what was actually necessary versus what may not require my immediate attention. Making that change allowed me to ease up on myself and subsequently my husband as well.

Another thing to remember about communication, is to be mindful of who you are communicating to. If you have an issue with your partner, talk to him/her. Don't talk to everyone else about what he or she did that bothered you. If you don't give them an opportunity to fix the problem, then you shouldn't complain if it becomes an ongoing issue. Also, it's important to protect your marriage. Once you start inviting other people in, you'll never be able to get rid of their opinions as it relates to your relationship.

Even though most people will tell you not to go to bed mad at your spouse, what I have learned in my marriage is that sometimes it's best to call it quits for the night and then revisit the issue in the morning. When we are tired and angry, the probability of us saying something that we will regret later is much higher. So acknowledge when you both just need to get some sleep and then start afresh. You'd be surprised how trivial some matters may seem the morning after. If the issue at hand is still a major problem once you have gotten some rest, at least you all can tackle the problem head-on with a clearer mindset and hopefully with a calmer temperament.

And please do not hold grudges. I know that can be easier said than done, but holding on to past discrepancies doesn't help either of you. Address the issues and then move on (I'm still working on this one myself)! Be sure to respect each other too. Once your partner has filled you in on how they feel about a particular matter, respect their wishes. Don't just listen to their thoughts and feelings; take mental notes and do your best to take them into consideration. Even in small matters, show your significant other that you care about how they feel—in most cases the behavior will be reciprocated.

The most important piece of advice that I will give you about communication is to make sure that you get uninterrupted time to communicate, aka quality time together (without your kids). This is something that Henry and I have taken seriously since the beginning of our marriage. We got pregnant seven months after tying the knot—meaning, we had very little time as just husband and wife before our older son made his debut into the world. I was twenty-six at the time, and Henry was twenty-seven years old. Most of our friends were out living their best lives, and meanwhile, we were new parents. Those first couple years of parenthood were pretty stressful for us—Jacob was colicky and didn't sleep through the night until he was almost two years old. However, in the midst of the biggest transition of our lives, we still made a conscious effort to spend quality time together. We made sure to get our date nights in and take a couple of trips a year; my parents would keep Jacob, and we got to take advantage of a few days here and there solo. I know that everyone may not have parents or in-laws who live locally. But find someone whom you can trust and depend on for childcare at least once a month (or as often as possible). It's so important to have time together where you can communicate and make sure you are on the same page. I cannot stress this point enough. Henry will agree that us making time for one another has been a total saving grace in our marriage. Which leads me to my next point...

Keep in mind, ladies, that open communication can be handy in other areas too, not just when discussing household chores or our kids. When it comes to matters of intimacy, some of us may shy away from being honest about what we want. Sometimes it's because we don't want to hurt our partner's feelings, other times we may be embarrassed, or it could be that we don't fully know ourselves. Regardless of the reason, I encourage you to drop your reservations and start a conversation with your spouse about the ways you all can best serve each other. When Henry and I were finally open and honest with one another, our intimacy reached new heights. Just think about how much better your love life will be once you clearly communicate your wants and needs. And don't be selfish, find out what they like too. Making them happy will bring you pleasure also.

If you aren't sure what your favorite things in the bedroom are, take the time to find out. You'll connect in a whole new way and feel closer both physically and emotionally (thank me later)!

Being connected physically and emotionally is imperative in any good relationship but being connected spiritually leads to *great* relationships. I know that we may have different religious beliefs, so I encourage you to connect spiritually with your spouse in whatever fashion suits your marriage. Regardless, do not skip this part—it's too important. I know we've heard "The family that prays together stays together" more times than we can probably count. However, I truly believe being evenly yoked with your significant other really can make a world of difference in your relationship. My husband and I have made a point to do devotions together. We try our best to read them together daily, but if we don't get an opportunity, we still do them individually. We like to use the Bible App. They have numerous different plans and lessons to choose from that are catered to pretty much any area of your life. Henry and I will take turns choosing which plan we want to read and then invite the other person. The Bible App allows us to comment back and forth in their "discussion" section; this encourages us to have dialogue about the scriptures that were referenced in whichever plan we are reading at the time. I love this feature personally because it helps us hold each other accountable. If one of us starts to fall off, the other person can see that and remind the other to make time to communicate with God on a daily basis. We motivate each other to stay on track, and it helps us to be on the same page spiritually, which is priceless.

Communicating with God both individually and together has had a major impact on our marriage. Bringing Him into our conversations as the head of our household has kept us going strong for more than ten years.

Another reason why being spiritually in accord with your partner is so important is because having a higher power to lean on when the going gets tough (which it will) can mean the difference between perseverance and calling it quits. In relationships, nobody is perfect—period! The sincerest man or the most loving woman can and will make mistakes. The bottom line is that no one relationship is perfect because there are no perfect people. When trials and tribulations come your way, you want to make sure that your marriage is on solid ground—otherwise, just like the house made out of sand, when the tides turn, your house will likely wash away.

Because we are not perfect and every one of us will undoubtedly make mistakes in our relationships, we have to have the space to be honest with our significant other, without judgment. Whether it's an affair, a substance-abuse problem, or a gambling issue, having spirituality is the ingredient that will pull you through. But you both have to be committed to God, yourselves, and each other in order to overcome calamity. Only a higher power can foster true forgiveness and redemption, which are necessary steps toward reconciliation.

In addition to 1 Corinthians 13:4–8, another Bible passage that my husband and I have meditated on during tough times is Romans 12:9–13. I promise I won't get all holier than thou on you all, but allow me to share these verses with you in their entirety:

"9 Love must be sincere. Hate what is evil; cling to what is good. 10 Be devoted to one another in love. Honor one another above yourselves. 11 Never be lacking in zeal, but keep your spiritual fervor, serving the Lord. 12 Be joyful in hope, patient in affliction, faithful in prayer. [13] Share with the Lord's people who are in need. Practice hospitality."

The Bible references the above behavior as "love in action." I love that description, because if we choose to be fully committed to someone, we have to love them unconditionally in spite of their faults. We have to be able to forgive ourselves also, because contrary to our own beliefs, we have faults too!

I want to be clear that both parties have to do the work. For a relationship to come out of the fire refined, both people involved have to be willing to be honest, forgive one another, and be devoted to moving forward regardless of past shortcomings.

I told you all in the introduction that we would have open and honest conversations. This is the part of the discussion where we accept that each relationship will be tested. The tests will come in different shapes and sizes and look and feel differently, depending on the circumstances. However, I will remind you here, that communication is the cornerstone of a strong relationship. When you can bare your soul to your spouse without judgment and retribution, your bond will only be strengthened and your marriage sustained.

After all, during our wedding ceremonies, each of us said some version of "I, _____, take thee, _____, to be my wedded wife/husband, to have and to hold, from this day forward, for better, for worse, for richer, for poorer, in sickness and in health, to love and to cherish, till death do us part, according to God's holy ordinance; and thereto I pledge thee my faith." It's not by coincidence that "for better or worse" or "through thick and thin" in some translations were included in traditional wedding vows. Someone somewhere knew that verbiage was necessary. Because no matter how much your care about someone or how enamored you may be with your mate, the two of you will experience pain and heartache—and it may not even be self-inflicted. There are couples who struggle with infertility or have to cope with the loss of a child. Unexpected unemployment and financial hardships will always take a toll. Kids who grow up and make poor decisions or fail to live up to their parents' expectations can be challenging as well.

Usually, when we first get married, we put our significant others on a pedestal. Then we tend to get caught up in trying to be perceived as #relationshipgoals. The problem with "relationship goals" is that no one truly knows what is behind the scenes in even what may seem to be the best of marriages (nor should they because your marriage is between you and the person you choose to marry; everyone else's thoughts and opinions should be irrelevant). So when life smacks us in the face, however she chooses to humble us, we have to be able to address and handle whatever the matter is at hand. More often than not, these circumstances will require faith—the mustard seed type.

All in all, open communication really can be the difference in our lives in general but especially our love lives. And it's the first step in creating healthy relationships and the key to unlocking the marriage you've always hoped for.

➤ Stop setting invisible expectations; be straightforward

Too often, we set invisible expectations for our significant others (and our other loved ones as well) and then become frustrated when they don't live up to our unspoken expectations. And most of the time, their actions are not intentional; the other person really didn't have a clue how we felt, which goes back to having open communication (see how communication is key!).

If you set clear expectations, by stating them to your spouse, there is no longer room for confusion or miscommunication. So what does being up front with your expectations look like?

Well, that can vary from person to person and from couple to couple (more on this topic later). For me, as I mentioned earlier, I choose to write out a honey-do list for my husband on the days that he's working from home. Early on in our relationship, I was annoyed that this was even necessary. In my mind, no one took the time to remind me of what needed to be done around the house—I felt we are all adults here; just do what needs to be done. And while that sounds good, in reality that did not work for my marriage. My husband expressed to me that when he knew what I expected of him, he stayed on course, preventing me from getting frustrated and him feeling like he wasn't meeting my expectations. This is an example of compromising. As women, we have to be open and listen when our mates express themselves to us. It doesn't matter if we agree or not, everyone needs the room to communicate (there's that word again) their feelings in a safe space.

Once I committed to providing my husband with my honey-do list for him, two things changed: He started meeting my expectations (because they were clearly stated), and I stopped resenting him for not just knowing what I wanted him to do. Setting straightforward expectations improved both of our quality of lives at home.

Every married couple has their own set of "relationship rules" as I like to call them. If you don't, you should develop some with your spouse. They can be as rigid or loose as you'd like, as long as you and your mate are on the same page.

I'm a strong believer in protecting your marriage ahead of time. What do I mean by that you may ask? I mean surround yourselves with couples who share the same values as you and your significant other. For Henry and me, that looks like having friends who are married believe in putting God first, then family, and everything else after that. We hang out with couples who we can learn from and be inspired by. We choose not to have too many single friends. Not because there's anything wrong with being single, but because single people and married folks have different mindsets—at least they should. Ultimately, no matter how proactive you try to be, temptations will likely still arise because the devil is real and wants to break up your union. But if you keep God first and in the midst of your relationship, your marriage can and will withstand the test of time. It won't always be easy, and at times your relationship will even be hard. However, all you can do is make an active decision every day to keep choosing your spouse.

This would be a good time to jot down some "rules" or boundaries that you would like for you and your partner to follow (if you haven't already).

By setting clear standards, you all will feel more comfortable knowing that you are on the same page. Whether discussing household chores, interactions with coworkers, or how you'd like to discipline your children, being transparent can only improve your chances of having a healthy relationship, which is what we are all striving for.

> **Figure out which communication style works best for your relationship**

I don't have to tell you that every couple is different; what works for one may not necessarily work for another. Have an open discussion with your partner and talk about your preferred method of communication. That may sound silly to some; why can't you just talk to each other, right? The reason why I wanted to highlight different communication styles is because my husband and I don't just talk to each other; we may communicate our feelings via text messages, email, or even handwritten letters.

Many years ago I realized that it was better for me to write out my feelings versus talk about them verbally. Sometimes in the midst of a heated debate or argument you don't think and say something that you wish you hadn't. So instead of talking verbally whenever something is bothering me, I choose to write my feelings down. Not only is it therapeutic for me to get my feelings out but it allows me the opportunity to really sort through my thoughts. That way, when I bring my concerns to Henry, I can communicate my feelings clearly. I won't get off topic and bring up things from the past; it gives me the power to convey the exact message that I want to get across to him. Also, taking the time to write down some of my emotions makes me realize when I am being petty or small minded myself.

Henry always jokes about how he knows he's "in trouble" when he gets an email from his wife. But on a serious note, we've used the written form of communication for a little over ten years now, and it works for our relationship. Of course, we aren't writing about every little thing—we don't have time for that. But if one of us truly is bothered, we will send a text message, email, or leave a letter for each other in a heartbeat.

On the flip side, we also make a point to do the same when we want to express our love and adoration for one another. I'll leave out a handwritten note telling Henry that I love him and can't wait for our next date night.

If I know he's had a long day, I may jot down a one-liner on a Post-it and leave it on the counter with a glass of Grand Marnier (one of his favorite liquors to drink). It's a small gesture, but it makes a major impact.

In the same way, he'll leave me a note with flowers or a piece of my favorite candy (he knows the way to my heart) to express his appreciation for all that I do for him and our boys. These are each different forms of communication, which show our love toward one other.

In addition, be sure to learn each other's love language(s). I feel loved when my husband gives me affirmations. Hearing that I look beautiful or that he noticed when I changed my hair makes me feel special. When he expresses appreciation for everything that I do to keep our household running smoothly, it makes me want to grind even harder. On the other hand, he likes to be connected physically—not only when it comes to romance but in general.

Whether we hold hands, I stroke his arm, or I brush my lips against his neck, these are all ways in which he is reminded that I love him and desire to be near him. When we take the time to learn our spouse's love language(s), our marriage benefits overall.

➤ Accept that men and women really are different

The saying "women are from Venus and men are from Mars" is really true! I'm certain that I'm not the only woman that feels this way. The things on the top of our priority list that we think need to be addressed or taken care of right away usually looks a bit different when we compare notes with our significant others. Men will say things like, "It will get taken care of;

don't stress yourself out!" While that sounds good, that statement is legitimately one of my biggest pet peeves. Because to me that "it will get taken care of" attitude usually means me taking care of whatever.

I'm the one who sorts through my kids' clothes to see what they can still fit versus what has been outgrown. To a mother, those types of things are important. To a father, as long as the children are breathing, fed, and clothed, they are fine.

Now I have to follow that statement up with, my husband is a phenomenal father. His dad hasn't been in his life since he was five years old. Yet, in spite of lacking a relationship with his own father, he goes above and beyond for our boys. However, his focus is making sure they are provided for and taken care of. So Henry is constantly grinding to create a solid foundation for us and figuring out ways to create generational wealth for his family.

While I appreciate his efforts every single day, this goes back to that bigger picture mind frame that I mentioned earlier. Ultimately, I'm thankful to have a husband that is concerned about setting our family up for success, but what that also means is that while he is planning for the future, I'm focused on our day-to-day routine. Both are equally important, but I had to realize that we are different and so are our priorities.

Once you accept that men and women really are different and so are our thought processes, you can immediately begin to release the notion that you will operate the same way.

➢ Don't settle, but always be willing to compromise

In the end, marriage is just one big compromise. The food we eat for dinner, the music we listen to in the car, which movie we watch, or what family activity we choose on the weekend, all boils down to compromising. If you choose to get married, this is a concept that I urge you to become familiar with.

You cannot marry someone and then expect that they are always going to want to do what you want to do or do things your way. It's not practical for one, and secondly, the point of joining one's life with another is to do just that—join your lives together. I'm not saying that you can never have an independent thought or take some me time for yourself. What I am saying is that you will have to give and take in order to have longevity in your marriage. So maybe you were in the mood for Mexican food, but you decide to go with Italian instead because that is what your partner wanted for dinner. No big deal in the grand scheme of things, right? Or decide to each get your own food from different places, whatever makes you happy. But do not expect your partner to cave to your preferences every single time, and that works both ways; you should not be expected to go along with what your spouse wants all of the time either. This is where clearly communicating your desires up front can cut down on frustration later. In the same regard, do not move forward with someone who you know you are not willing to compromise with. Also be able to determine what is worth compromising and what is not.

Never compromise your self-worth or dignity for anyone else. Realize that more than likely if a man tells you that he doesn't believe in marriage, he means that. Don't waste time trying to convince him otherwise or compromising your standards to appease him.

Earlier in our conversation, I mentioned taking stock of what you are willing to compromise on in a relationship and what was a deal breaker for you. The reason why this step is one you should not put on the back burner is because you do not want to wind up in a situation where someone showed you exactly who they were initially and you then kept moving forward and ignored all of the red flags just to find out that they were in fact who they told you they were up front.

If I could stress any one point to women who may be seeking marriage but have not made it there yet, it would be to pay attention to whom you seriously consider starting a life with.

Now are there some cases where a man may have fooled you into thinking they were one way when in all actuality they were totally different? Yes!

However, if we are honest with ourselves, most of the time we did notice little things here and there that did not sit well with us, yet we kept moving forward in the relationship anyway. When everything hits the fan, we cannot then be surprised that our partner never changed or became who we hoped he would be. Obviously, people can change. But ultimately it has to be their desire to change in order for real change to take place.

You should never pursue a relationship based on who you hope a person will become. If you are not completely satisfied with the person as they are right now, you will set yourself up for disappointment later.

For all of the married ladies out there, you've already taken the plunge. If you have tried to have open communication and really done your part everywhere else and your partner is unwilling to work with you or compromise, then you have a decision to make. Don't settle for less than you deserve for any reason. I know that may be a hard pill to swallow. You may say that you have kids to think about, or maybe financially you don't think you would be able to make it without him. But what's the alternative? Staying in a marriage where you are unhappy and underappreciated? You have to love yourself enough to know that you only have one life to live, and life truly is short. Don't spend your time fighting for a relationship or a person who isn't exerting the same energy to fight for you.

I will never tell anyone to get a divorce; only you can make that decision for yourself. I believe in families staying together and weathering the storms of life in unison. But I am also an advocate for people experiencing true happiness, and if your marriage does not bring you joy more than it brings you pain, you've got to do what's right for you and your family.

If you are happily married, keep putting in the work day in and day out—it's not a sprint; it's a marathon. Make sure you are taking the proper tools with you along the way so that your relationship can make the distance.

Mommy Dearest

M otherhood, without a doubt is one of the toughest jobs on the planet. To carry a child inside you and then birth them, nurse them, and raise them to be self-sufficient human beings is nothing short of a miracle. While children are one of God's biggest blessings, raising them requires a level of patience and understanding that only God can provide.

Even though I always knew that I wanted to be a mother at some point in my life, I usually envisioned myself getting acclimated in my profession first and then beginning a family a couple of years into my already successful career. That's the funny thing about our plans for ourselves—we tend to think that we know what is best for us, but ultimately God *always* knows better.

I graduated in May of 2012, with my doctor of pharmacy degree (PharmD) from Hampton University School of Pharmacy; my life took off directly after that. I got married that June, passed my board exams in July, and then began working in August. My husband and I closed on our house in September, and in January of 2013, I was pregnant. I only worked one year full time and then immediately went down to part time after our older son, Jacob, was born. So I know the feeling of trying to navigate everything all at once and life seemingly changing in an instant. Plus, I felt alone at times because we were one of the first couples to get married and have children out of all of our friends. Most of our close friends are just now having kids; we started at twenty-six as I mentioned before—it was definitely an adjustment for me, as motherhood can feel like a lot all at once. But with time, you get into a routine and find your own rhythm. I'm still figuring it out as I go, and every time I feel like I have a handle on things, something changes. Regardless, I keep trying to be the best mother that I can be for my children.

Ultimately, as a wife, mother, and young professional, all you can do is the best that *you* can do. Rely on your support system and don't be afraid or embarrassed to ask for help. That's a mistake that I made with Jacob, and because of it I suffered quietly with mild postpartum depression for several months after he was born.

Motherhood was something that I had always dreamed of, and as a little girl, I would play house and pretend that my baby doll was real. I have to laugh at my younger self now as I realize that being a mother is so much more than feeding, burping, and changing a baby's diaper.

So often we are sucked into believing that motherhood is just like a Huggies commercial—you are happy and so full of joy all of the time, right? Wrong! On my best day, I am not happy all day long. Even if my children are acting well behaved, there is still the stress of making sure that they are ready for school and that they're on time for their after-school activities, and then there's the hustle and bustle of our dinner-time and bath routine. The bottom line is that nothing could ever truly prepare you for motherhood.

No matter how many stories you hear or how much advice you get, when you are actually the one responsible for keeping a tiny human alive and then raising that tiny human to become a self-sufficient adult, there's not a manual in the world that could do the role of mother justice.

➤ What type of mother are you?

There are all different types of mothers in the world; I've learned that I'm more of a "helicopter mom." I have zero shame in that fact. Since the day I found out I was pregnant with Jacob, like most mothers, I worried about him. I wanted to make sure that I did all of the right things and ate all of the right food. I prayed over his unborn life incessantly.

Once he arrived, nothing changed. He's almost eight years old, and I'm still extremely protective of him. I'm always thinking a worst-case scenario and trying to prevent it from happening at all costs.

Honestly, I know that my overbearing and overprotective demeanor really just drives me nuts and doesn't necessarily do him any favors either. Regardless, he still has never played outside unattended or walked to the school bus stop by himself. I've had other mothers comment on how I should "loosen up" or be a bit more liberal. It doesn't faze me either way. You want to know why? Because I realized what type of mother I was years ago, embraced that fact, and kept it moving. I carried my children, birthed them, and it's my job to raise them how I see fit. I'm not the "cool mom" or the one trying to be their BFF. I'm fine with that. Not that there is anything wrong with those types of moms. It's just that I don't fit into those categories; nor do I try to.

Oftentimes when other moms give me advice, I evaluate whether or not it's relevant to my children and then choose to take it or leave it from there.

As a mother of two young Black boys, I feel that my mothering style is intensified. If we learned nothing else over the course of 2020, we did learn (or finally began to admit) that mothers of Black children really do have additional reasons to fear for our kids. This is a harsh truth that we've come to realize and sadly accept.

My kids are growing every day, and I feel like the time is only ticking. Eventually, people will stop thinking they are cute and will feel threatened by them or be suspicious of them. Not because they've done anything wrong or outwardly offended anyone. The color of their skin alone puts them at greater risk. The thought sometimes keeps me up at night. I wonder how they are treated at school by their teachers and peers.

When Jacob was five years old, he randomly asked me out of the blue one night after bath time, "Do you love Joshua more than me because he's white?" I was stunned. I literally lost my breath for a few seconds. At that point we had not had any conversations about race or ethnicity with Jacob (we were forced to have "the talk" with him in 2020, much earlier than we ever intended to).

My initial thought was what happened to him that caused him to correlate the additional attention that Joshua received at that time because he was a baby to the fact that his skin was lighter? I immediately began to explain to Jacob that first Joshua was not white—he was just lighter skinned. Then I assured him that complexion had absolutely zero to do with the fact that Joshua may require additional attention because he was a baby and less independent than Jacob at the time. Last, I loved on him and told him that he had beautiful brown skin just like mommy. That conversation is forever etched in my mind and one that totally broke my heart.

When I inquired what made him ask me that, he said he didn't know. I was left wondering what ever prompted that conversation to begin with. That is just one example of how the stressors of motherhood can be amplified when you have children of color.

In addition to the regular growing pains and concerns, there is a whole other element at play. I do not highlight this point to make any mother feel bad; that's never my intention.

However, if you are reading this book and have the privilege of not being able to relate, acknowledge your privilege and do your part to raise children who are aware of their privilege as well. If we don't start having more candid conversations with our children all the way around, nothing will ever change.

Now back to my original topic—whatever type of mother you are, be proud and embrace it. Be proud of yourself. Don't let anyone else make you feel less than because you don't do this or you do that!

Perfect segue to my next piece of advice...

➤ Let's stop comparing ourselves

Never compare yourself to other moms. Do whatever works best for you and your family. Be willing to take advice, but ultimately the only opinions that matter are yours and your children's father's. As long as you all are in accord, you guys will be fine! I think in general we live in a world that encourages comparisonitis. I know that may not be a real word, but it's definitely a real thing. Every day people post themselves living their "best lives" on social media.

We then scroll through our various feeds and internalize everything we see. I'm guilty of this too. I've seen mothers who post themselves doing all of these cool and creative activities with their kids. I'd then beat myself up for always doing the same basic activities with my kids or worse not having time to do activities with them at all.

My husband usually then reminds me of all of the ways that I'm an awesome mother to our children. He would also scold me for even comparing myself to begin with and insist that I can't compare myself to someone whose lifestyle may be totally different than mine.

For years Henry and I were shielded from social media and its negative effects because neither of us were on it. When I initially joined Facebook, it was 2005, and I was just beginning my freshman year at Hampton University. It was my first time dabbling in any type of social media as I had never used Myspace, BlackPlanet, or anything else that was previously available. At the time, you had to be in college and have an official login to be able to join Facebook.

I believe, when this platform was initially created, it was meant for good. This particular site made it easy to stay in contact with all of your high school friends and keep tabs on one another. It was a cool way to stay connected, even if you were spread out all over the country, attending different colleges and universities. But like anything else, what Facebook was initially intended for morphed into something else in its entirety. Before long everyone was welcomed on the site, and people realized they had a megaphone to spout whatever crossed their mind, whether it was positive or not.

Usually, people are using social media for good—whether they are staying in contact with friends or family or spreading uplifting messages. Of course, there are always those who only use it to perpetrate or say things to people that they would never say to anyone in person. But in most cases, folks are using social media appropriately.

I saw a statistic somewhere recently that cited how social media was one of the top five reasons that people divorce nowadays. Henry and I had both gotten off of Facebook before we started dating, and I had never joined Twitter. Snapchat, TikTok, and everything else was nonexistent at the time. We believe the absence of social media was beneficial to our relationship in the beginning.

Don't get me wrong, I realize that most people are on some form of social media at this point, and I am not telling you that in order to have a successful relationship you must delete all of your social media accounts. However, I am telling you to be mindful of the effect that social media has on your relationship.

In 2019, when we opened our small business, The Prescription Shoppe, a full-service community, independent pharmacy, that is locally owned and family operated, we realized that we would finally have to cave and join the social media world that prior to our business venture we had successfully avoided. To go almost ten years with zero form of social media in this day and age is pretty commendable in my book (literally, LOL). Once we joined Facebook, Twitter, and Instagram, I was exposed to things I had always heard about for years from close friends but never really experienced myself personally.

Ultimately, social media can definitely be used for good, but it can also cause us to feel inadequate or less than. As mothers we have to vow to ourselves and each other that we will stop comparing ourselves to one another and shaming other mothers for doing things a little differently than we may choose to do them.

When we lift each other up and use each other as a resource, it prevents drama, and we all win. Choose to be supportive of other moms and cheer them on, not judge, critique, or envy them. You will feel better mentally and emotionally, and you will have one less thing to worry about because, let's face it, as mothers we already have enough on our plates.

➢ Make time for memories

Making memories with my children is something that I care deeply about, but struggle to actually do. There are several factors, including having a full schedule and being tired, that usually prevent me from creating those super memorable moments with my boys. At some point all mothers will have to evaluate what really matters in life. It's easy to get caught up in our everyday routines and sometimes not legitimately make time for the people and things we love most.

We are all guilty of this. But the reality is that everything doesn't have to be some major event for it to be memorable. Oftentimes, it's the little things that make us laugh till we cry or an impromptu dance session that our kids will cherish most. They will remember how we helped them with their homework, fixed their favorite food, and let them eat popcorn before dinner (on occasion).

As parents, and mothers especially, we put so much pressure on ourselves to be this superwoman. Of course, I'm a believer in the fact that all moms are real-life superheroes who possess supernatural powers, but that doesn't mean we have to kill ourselves to live up to some image of the perfect mom. And definitely not if it comes at the expense of our children or our mental health.

We do need to decide that we are going to take the time to soak up those giggles and snuggles as long as we can though. If there's one thing that I've heard repeatedly about motherhood that I've found to be true, it's the fact that kids really do grow in the blink of an eye. I feel like I just had Jacob, and now Joshua is already almost four. My husband and I spent so much of Josh's baby years laying the foundation for The Prescription Shoppe and then grinding to get our business off the ground that I sometimes feel as though I traded a special season to pursue entrepreneurship. When I reflect on the decision to start a small business when we had young children (Jacob was five and Josh was a one-year-old at the time), I'm torn.

I'm tremendously thankful to be a small-business owner of a pretty successful business. In order to turn that dream into a reality I had to sacrifice some quality time with my kids. At times, that was a really hard pill for me to swallow. After all, I just talked about how our babies grow too quickly. Mom guilt is a very real emotion that can totally consume us.

However, as much as we love our children and are blessed to experience motherhood as some women struggle to conceive, we are more than mothers. We are people with feelings, dreams, and aspirations—becoming a mother shouldn't change that!

➤ Don't lose yourself in motherhood

Being a mother is *awesome*; I love my little boys to the moon and back. But I have to remind myself daily that I am more than a mother. I am a wife, daughter, sister, friend, pharmacist, small-business owner, sorority sister, board member, community leader, and now author. As I previously mentioned, and just like a lot of you currently reading this book, I wear a lot of hats.

The reason why I am an advocate for women being involved with additional commitments outside of the home (not necessarily working but community service of some sort) is because our babies don't stay babies. If we devote all of our time to motherhood, when our kids grow up and start spending more time with their friends, where does that leave us? So often you see women totally lose themselves in motherhood and then look up one day and not know who they are, what they like, and what interests them.

Stay active in your community or church or whatever ensures that you have an identity outside of your kids. Continue to find time for your hobbies and things that you enjoy doing (more on self-care later). You will not always have time, but make sure that once a day, week, or month you do something for you (as often as you possibly can). There are people who will say that sounds selfish and speak of how "good moms devote themselves to their kids." I agree, being devoted to your kid(s) is great, but if you don't find time to take care of your mental and emotional well-being, you can't be your best for your children!

So I encourage whatever you need to do to stay in touch with yourself and who you are—because the truth is, our children will get older and have their own hobbies, friends, and eventually their own lives. Of course, they will still always need their mothers but not in the same ways. Another reason why I believe moms should have a life outside of motherhood is because it sets an example for their kids. Whether you have girls or boys, it's important for them to see that their mothers are involved in things as well. Again, you may be a stay-at-home mom (that's a full-time job in itself); there's nothing wrong with that. You are bringing value to your home.

However, I encourage you to join a ministry at church or volunteer for a nonprofit organization that you are passionate about. There are other ways to have a life that doesn't revolve around our roles as mothers. Daughters then have the opportunity to see their mothers in a different light. Yes, you are their mom, but you are also fulfilled in other areas of your life. Your sons can appreciate witnessing firsthand how valuable women are to not only raise their children but also have an impact outside of their homes.

It was really important to me that my boys grow up having a mutual respect for both of their parents. So while I did only work part time, I insisted on still having an impact on my profession. I realize that I was blessed to be able to do both—being there for my children while also participating in my field and using a degree that I had worked extremely hard for.

I know that everyone may not be in a position to do both or may not even have the desire to do both. Regardless, having interests that are not directly related to you being a mom also creates space for you to have a break every once in a while.

Eventually, when you reach the point where your kids are self-sufficient, you will know exactly who you are because you never lost yourself to begin with.

Working Woman

F or years, women have been made to feel that we should be content with taking the more "traditional" route of being a wife and mother. Thankfully, over the past few decades, we have seen a shift in how women are viewed in the workforce. Instead of our thoughts and ideas being dismissed or undervalued, women are taking on leadership roles and occupying positions of power. Glass ceilings are being shattered all over the place, and women are finally getting the praise and recognition that we deserve. Let's face it, women have always been essential to the growth and stability of our economy. Now, we are given more opportunities, sitting in boardrooms where decisions are being made. And in the fields that are lagging behind when it comes to inclusion and diversity in the workplace, women are building their own tables and taking charge.

Whether you make the decision that you are going to be a career woman, a stay-at-home mom, or do both, remember that your passions should be front and center and that you have the freedom to create the life that you want for yourself.

➢ Women with vision

It's been said that little girls with dreams become women with vision; I could not agree more. It is so important to teach our girls and young women to start dreaming *big*, now! You are never too young or too old to have a dream and then pursue it.

For me, deciding to pursue a career in the field of pharmacy came about somewhere around my junior year in high school. I then asked a community pharmacist who worked inside one of our local grocery stores if she'd agree to let me complete my senior year internship with her.

I was born and raised in Bowie, Maryland, fifteen minutes from Annapolis and thirty minutes from D.C. (without traffic). Instead of going to the public high school that I was zoned for, I attended another high school within my division after testing into their math and science program. Even though I've always loved reading and writing with a passion, I wanted to pursue a career in the health care field. My interest in the profession of pharmacy specifically stemmed from watching my father work in the pharmaceutical industry my entire life. My sister, Jasmine, and I were aware that we were living a privileged lifestyle. We had two parents in our home who both did extremely well for themselves. My dad worked thirty-three years for Bristol Myers Squibb, and my mother worked for the National Institute of Health (NIH) in radiology. I knew that when I grew up, I wanted to have a profession too—one that would afford me the opportunity to create a similar lifestyle for my own children.

Once I settled on becoming a pharmacist, I then took steps toward turning my dream into a reality. Growing up in Prince George's County (PG County), I was blessed to be exposed to many African American professionals who lived very comfortable lifestyles, so it wasn't hard for me to imagine myself standing behind the counter in a pharmacy, wearing a white coat. It is so true that representation really does matter, and for children of color, seeing people who look like them succeed can make all the difference.

Attending a high school that focused heavily on Science, Technology, Engineering & Math (STEM) programs also helped me to further my quest by allowing me to choose my own senior internship. The pharmacist who graciously agreed to let me shadow her two or three days a week during my senior year left an undeniable impression on me.

I watched as she cared for her patients by applying her knowledge to help them improve their quality of life. She was always professional, compassionate, and assertive—all attributes I hoped to embody once I had the opportunity to don my own white coat.

I was just a girl with a dream who had no idea where life was going to take me, but I made a conscious effort to make choices that would ultimately lead me to who I wanted to become—a woman with vision!

According to the *Merriam-Webster Dictionary*, the word "vision" in this context equals a thought, concept, or object formed by the imagination.

We each have the ability to envision what we want for ourselves, both professionally and personally. Some of us get super excited about an idea and then never follow up with action to turn our idea(s) into a reality. In addition to vision, we need action—even the Bible talks about how faith without works is dead (James 2:17).

You have to decide that your concept or thought process is worth pursuing. Once you do, you have to start putting your money where your mouth is. Make a game plan to determine how you will bring your idea to fruition. Too often, people know where they want to end up but don't have a clue how to get there. Can you just wing it? Absolutely! However, having a plan will usually make for a smoother ride without the additional stress of being unprepared.

Most of us have probably experienced a moment in our lives at least once or twice where maybe we procrastinated and were not as prepared as we would have liked for our test, presentation, or job interview. Due to our lack of preparation, we were likely more flustered and potentially even distracted because we knew we were not on top of our game.

If you are seriously considering pursing a new career path or owning your first home or launching your own small business, you need to start evaluating things now. Do some investigation and figure out how prepared you currently are and any necessary steps that you need to take in order to make "it" happen—whatever you desire to accomplish. Use your passion to create what you want in life, then don't let anyone deter you from chasing your dreams and pursuing your goals.

➤ Set goals; track your progress

I read a quote recently by Katherine Paterson that said, "A dream without a plan is just a wish." No matter where you are in life, it's never too late to set new goals; once you do be sure to track your progress. Earlier in this chapter, I mentioned how little girls with dreams become women with vision—that's true! But I also want to emphasize that little girls are not the only ones with dreams.

Even if you didn't have it all figured out at seventeen years old (I didn't either; I just had an idea), and maybe you still don't know, that's totally fine. I want to clarify that while I did choose to pursue the profession of pharmacy early on, it still took me several years of strategic planning, hard work, and perseverance to actually achieve my goal. Some people are still finding their passion well into their thirties and forties, and there's nothing wrong with that.

Thankfully, I do love my career and have been able to make an impact on my profession. I could have just as easily put in all of this time and energy to realize that pharmacy wasn't for me. I have a few classmates who discovered that to be true for them post-graduation.

There may be some of you who are reading this book right now who are questioning your career choices. Whether you are looking for your next big break or feel totally fulfilled in your current role, it's always a good idea to set goals for yourself—both professionally and personally. Once you establish short-term and long-term goals for yourself, don't stop there. It's always good to chart out an expected time frame of when you would like to have accomplished each one of your goals. Some people even create vision boards for what they hope to achieve over the next five or ten years.

Having a game plan allows us to stay focused and to stay the course. In life, things will always come up and maybe you have to make some adjustments from time to time and that's okay. As you have a general idea of where you are going, you can take active steps to prepare for what you are hoping to eventually accomplish. And remember, goals are not only for major life aspirations like maybe owning your own home or starting your own business—little goals like trying to be more disciplined in your daily approach are just as important.

Something that I have personally always struggled with is being on time, and having small children has made it that much harder for me.

I remember my freshman year in college when one of our administrators used to tell us repeatedly, "To be early is to be on time, to be on time is to be late, and to be late is unacceptable!"

That is a mantra that has always stuck with me no matter how many times I may fail to actually implement the practice in my daily life. Recently, I have been getting better with being on time because I took personal stock of my own patterns and realized that I wasn't giving myself enough time in the mornings to get myself and the boys ready for the day. Instead of getting frustrated when Joshua decides to run around and play when I am trying to get him ready for camp, I started allotting additional time for his behavior.

So now instead of having just enough time to get ready, I started waking up earlier to give myself an additional forty minutes for any potential shenanigans that may occur during our morning routine. It seems like a small adjustment, but it has made a world of difference. When my mornings start out stressful, it often sets the tone for the rest of my day. If I am scrambling all morning, I usually feel overwhelmed and the potential for me to be off my game at work increases. In my profession, I cannot afford to make mistakes or be distracted.

We each have areas where we can improve, so put together a game plan of what you need to do to have better results. After you start implementing your game plan, check in with yourself periodically to determine whether or not your game plan is in fact working and beneficial. When we track our progress, it gives us the opportunity to evaluate, critique, and ultimately make necessary adjustments. None of us has time to waste; therefore you want to work smarter and not harder.

That's why evaluation is so crucial. If we don't make time to confirm that our method is having a positive effect, we could waste our time tracking in the wrong direction. And even if you are not on the wrong path altogether, you could find that there is a more direct route.

Here's where I'll repeat just for emphasis (and for those who may not have tried being more intentional when it comes to charting your progress), setting goals and tracking your progress is essential to your success!

➤ Success is in the eye of the beholder

I believe that just like beauty is in the eye of the beholder, so is success. Your version of success may look very different than mine—ultimately, who cares if we are both happy and feel fulfilled in our respective lives? I'll give the same advice here that I gave when discussing motherhood: I repeat, do not compare yourselves! Whether we are talking about relationships, motherhood, or our careers, women and men tend to compare our lives. Once you accept that you are happy with yourself, you'll find that it doesn't matter how happy someone else may be in their lives.

We've all heard the common phrase "the grass looks greener on the other side." The part we usually tend to forget is that if our neighbor's grass truly is greener, their water bill is probably higher too. I sometimes have to remind myself just like I do my seven-year-old, "Focus on yourself!" When I'm so busy pursuing my dreams and working toward my goals, that leaves very little time for me to judge someone else or compare myself to anyone else.

Another saying we've heard a million times is that "everything that glitters isn't gold!" I think we have all found this to be true. Every one of you reading this book right now knows someone who is constantly posting how great their lives are, only for folks to find out that their life was really in shambles behind the scenes.

Everyone wants to "do it for the gram," and the "likes," but what about just doing it for you? Take a moment to think about whether or not you would still be happy in your career if you didn't get acknowledgment or applause. If folks weren't "liking" your life, would you? Once you can answer that question truthfully to yourself, you'll know how to move forward.

If success for you is a big house and a nice vehicle, good for you—go for it! If your idea of success isn't that, great—do you! We have to stop shaming each other for having different ideas of success. Whatever makes you happy and feel accomplished is what you should celebrate. At times, I've celebrated just getting out of the bed in the morning. We have to acknowledge our small wins just as much, if not more than the big ones.

Oftentimes, it's the day in and day out grind that builds our character and grit. It's the low moments where we have to persevere and rise to the occasion that really shows who we are. So we should never take those seasons of our lives for granted.

When you're in those low or challenging moments or even when you're experiencing high points, be sure to surround yourself with people who will cheer you on either way. We talked about the importance of surrounding yourselves with likeminded individuals earlier when discussing the effect that your friend circle can have on your marriage or romantic relationships—the same is true when you think about your professional career and life in general.

It's been said that "birds of a feather flock together." I have to say that I tend to agree with that statement. I'm not saying that people only ever hang out with folks who are exactly like them, but I am saying that we usually gravitate toward people with whom we have things in common.

I've always tried to be intentional about my friend group. I'm not a fan of drama, and I prefer to be with people who will build me up and motivate me to be the best version of myself. After all, if you are not spending time with people who will hold you accountable and push you, are your current relationships really serving you? And not just serving you but allowing you to serve others? When you find your core group of ladies or people in general, you'll know. They won't envy you or talk behind your back, they will celebrate your wins in life truly and encourage you when you need it most.

So as you pursue your version of success, whatever that looks like for you, make sure that you go to bat with a team that is going to support you along your journey.

➤ Life-work balance is nonnegotiable

I cannot stress the importance of creating a life-work balance enough. If you don't, it *will* eventually catch up to you. And when it does, it usually comes in the form of some type of nervous breakdown. Whether you experience depression, anxiety, insomnia, or your overall health just starts declining—there is always a connection between stress and our mental, physical, emotional, and spiritual well-being.

This is not the part where I act like I am above struggling with the issue of having a healthy life-work balance—I think that many of us have been guilty of putting ourselves on the back burner more than we should. Unfortunately, I know the struggle all too well and have been known to have a serious case of "superwoman syndrome." Superwoman syndrome usually occurs when a woman neglects herself and strives to achieve perfection in every aspect of her life while measuring her success or failure in terms of tangible outcomes.

A perfect example of me having a moment that confirmed that I wasn't making enough time for myself was Father's Day weekend of 2021. That Saturday we celebrated Juneteenth, the oldest-known celebration commemorating the end of slavery in the United States.

Juneteenth celebrates June 19, 1865, when General Granger made his way to Galveston, Texas, and brought news that the remaining enslaved people should be set free—effective immediately. Finally, two years after Abraham Lincoln declared the Emancipation Proclamation, the rest of the people of color were informed of their newfound freedom. And in 2021, President Biden officially made Juneteenth a federal holiday. As a result, my husband and I decided to close our store for the day instead of being open our usual weekend business hours from 9:00 a.m. to 2:00 p.m.

We had been invited to participate in Williamsburg's inaugural Juneteenth event, which included a car parade, music, games, speeches, and a host of other activities to acknowledge the true history of this country. Having this celebration gave our community an opportunity to reflect on and address how we could continue to make progress as it relates to social justice, economic, and financial equality. We were excited to attend this event and celebrate as a family, representing The Prescription Shoppe in the car parade. My husband and I also wanted to take advantage of this occasion to start teaching our children the importance of knowing their own history—even if they did not necessarily learn about it in school!

We had a wonderful time at the Juneteenth celebration and followed it up with a relaxing Father's Day. After enjoying our day together as a family, my husband went to watch the Atlanta Hawks take on the Philadelphia 76ers to determine which team would advance to the NBA Eastern Conference Finals with a couple of his buddies—the NBA playoffs were in full swing. We got the boys settled before he went out that evening, and Jacob and Joshua were in bed early that night (not a usual occurrence in the Ranger household). I then took a hot shower, drank my nightly chamomile tea with valerian root, and decided to watch a show or two before my husband made it back home.

I wasn't watching anything particularly deep or dramatic; I decided to go with *Grown-ish*, a spin-off of the popular show *Black-ish* on ABC. Toward the end of the second thirty-minute episode, I burst into tears. Not because the show had been sad but because I realized that I had *really* enjoyed that hour of just watching somewhat meaningless television.

All of a sudden, it hit me that I literally could not remember the last time that I just sat down to watch a show, movie, or anything other than having CNN or ESPN playing in the background—either by myself or with my husband. We had been on the go so much the early part of 2021, administering roughly 3,500 COVID-19 vaccines from the end of January up until the beginning of June. That may not sound like a lot for the major chains, but for a small, independent community pharmacy with a staff of five people total, it was pretty monumental. In the midst of our COVID-19 vaccine distribution, we had several other things taking place in our lives, both personally and professionally.

We were asked to participate with our staff in the 2021 *Dancing with the Williamsburg Stars* to represent our small business, The Prescription Shoppe. This event has been long standing within our community, and we were slated as one of the premier teams to dance for the twelfth year of the show. *Dancing with the Williamsburg Stars* is an annual fundraiser that benefits two charities—Big Brothers Big Sisters and Literacy for Life. Each year influential people in our community are invited to participate and charged with raising money for these two great charities. This year, 2021, was the first time the show included local small businesses instead of individuals. Also, instead of being live, the show was pre-recorded—another result of COVID-19. So while we were prepping for our yearly inventory and preparing to administer COVID-19 vaccines, we were also learning a dance routine from our personal choreographer. The style of dance that was chosen for our team, DANCE THERxAPY, was ballroom dancing. While ballroom dancing was assigned to us, we were able to choose the song that we were to dance to. My husband and I are *huge* fans of the Broadway show, *Hamilton*; Henry surprised me with tickets for my thirtieth birthday, and we caught the train up to New York to see the play at the Richard Rogers Theater in 2017.

So naturally, we chose "The Schuyler Sisters" as the song we would dance to as a team. It was perfect because we had one guy and three ladies, just like that particular scene in the play (YouTube our performance for your entertainment)!

We learned our entire routine from prerecorded footage from our choreographer who had some underlying health concerns that put him at a greater risk if he were to contract COVID-19.

Our performance was a hit, and all of our patients and customers loved seeing us in our getups as we danced a samba,

West Coast swing, and a cha-cha. When all is said and done, we raised almost twenty thousand dollars in three months and walked away with the Fan Favorite Award—the award given to the team with the most individual votes.

Personally, I had been going back and forth to Maryland every chance I got to support my older sister, Jasmine, who was undergoing chemotherapy treatments for triple-negative breast cancer at the time. Jasmine was only thirty-nine years old when she was diagnosed in June of 2020.

My mother was a twenty-one-year breast-cancer survivor and a three-year ovarian-cancer survivor at this point. Unfortunately, the BRCA gene mutation runs in our family.

My sister and I each had a fifty-fifty chance, independent of one another, to inherit the BRCA gene mutation from my mother.

Jasmine tested positive, and I tested negative. Because my sister tested positive, she had to see a genetic counselor, an oncologist, and a team of doctors to monitor her potential risk for developing either breast cancer or ovarian cancer. The BRCA gene mutation significantly increases your chances for developing either type of cancer before the age of fifty. It had taken a few years for my sister to decide that she'd rather take a more proactive approach. Although she was originally scheduled to have a prophylactic double mastectomy and reconstruction on March 27, 2020, the country shutdown due to COVID-19, and her elective surgery was postponed.

When she had her next mammogram in June of 2020, they found a lump that wasn't present when she had her previous mammogram in December of 2019. Thankfully, she knew her BRCA status and was having a mammogram and a breast MRI, alternating every six months. Because of her rigorous testing, she was diagnosed early while still stage two. Her physicians immediately put together a game plan which included a double mastectomy and reconstruction in August of 2020 and then five months of chemotherapy (ladies, please be proactive with your health and get tested if you have a family history for anything but especially breast or ovarian cancer as early detection can literally save lives). We were all so proud of how hard she fought and how gracious she was during her entire journey. Instead of complaining, Jasmine, chose to uplift other women in her support group. So although I had been back and forth quite a bit, when her last treatment took place on January 29, 2021, I made sure that I was there to celebrate with her.

Needless to say, there had been an awful lot on my plate in addition to keeping up with The Prescription Shoppe, facilitating virtual learning, and dealing with all of the other stressors that 2020 presented us with. It was like I had been moving in fast-forward motion for a year and had never really taken a moment to think about how much of a mental and emotional toll everything that I was dealing with had on me.

As I found myself sobbing that night of Father's Day, I understood in an instant that no matter how much I was dealing with, it was *never* okay for me to completely neglect myself or my own needs. Right then, in that moment, I decided that

I wouldn't let another several months pass me by without taking time for me.

I'm sure that I am not the only wife, mother, or working woman to have an experience like this. In fact, I'm almost certain that this is not an isolated issue that is unique to me.

So today, right now, decide with me that you won't let your career, your family, or your nonstop schedule prevent you from addressing your own needs and taking the time to invest in yourself. Agree to take a few minutes or as much time as you can afford every day to do something that makes you happy. No matter how big or small, just this simple gesture can have a *major* impact on your mental health and overall well-being.

In addition to taking time for yourself, you have to make your health a priority. At the end of the day, if your health declines, it will impact your ability to take on your daily tasks and duties. Trust me when I say that I know how hard it can be to incorporate exercise into your weekly routine. So many times I have promised myself that I was going to get up early to work out, and then I hit the snooze button five times and had to forgo my workout for the day. Most of us have been in a rut at some point where we are not getting as much physical activity as we should be—if any at all. Again, as wives, mothers, and women with careers or who are staying active in our community, it can legitimately be a struggle to find the time to workout. Whether it's because we don't have time or we are just too tired, there's always a reason, and in most cases, it's a valid one. However, when we think about what is truly important, what's the alternative? If we neglect our health, we won't have it. I cannot tell you how many times I have seen patients who have to add additional prescription medication to their in some cases already extensive medication list because they were unwilling to incorporate lifestyle changes.

A quote that we have up on one of the walls in The Prescription Shoppe is, "Your health is an investment, not an expense!" That statement could not be truer. We have to invest in ourselves, ladies, especially if we want to continue to be around to really enjoy all of the fruits of our labor.

I have had to have a few "come to Jesus" moments with myself to make sure that I am making time for physical activity. I have also had to be way more conscious about what I am putting into my mouth.

While I have never had a terrible diet, I have always struggled with my portion sizes and of course my love of carbs and sweets. But even with all of my inconsistencies when it comes to diet and exercise, I keep trying. I encourage you to do the same even if you have had a few setbacks of your own. And it doesn't have to be completing a triathlon—just going for a thirty-minute walk a few times a week goes a long way.

Not only will you be getting your steps in but you will also be getting some fresh air, which gives you a chance to clear your mind and center your spirit. Never take for granted the positive impact that Mother Nature can have on your psyche and emotional well-being.

By investing in yourself first, you will then be in a position to give your very best to your family and loved ones. Remember that no matter how successful you may become, all of it means nothing if you are not surrounded by love.

No amount of material possessions or accolades will ever be able to make you feel completely fulfilled. We are human, and it is our nature to love and be loved. With that being said, I encourage you to invest time in those you love as often as possible.

Whether it's spending time with your spouse, playing a game with your kids, or snuggling up with your fur baby. The joy that we experience in these moments are usually the things that can get us through our day-to-day struggles and stressors.

Maintaining a life-work balance is crucial to ensuring that we are living an overall balanced life.

Legacy Matters

We all want to be successful in life while we are still living, but don't stop there. Leave behind a legacy by making contributions to things and causes bigger than yourself. Put your stamp on the world so that people will know you were here long after you are gone—when all is said and done, I want to feel like my life mattered and know that I fulfilled my purpose.

➢ Are you making power moves?

Making "power moves" will look differently for each of us, depending on our career goals and our personal goals. However, we can all agree that if we are not currently making any preparations for our future, we will likely be playing catch-up later. It is never too early to start planning for your retirement. None of us wants to be in a position where we are forced to work for the rest of our lives because we were ill prepared. If we plant the seeds now, we will be able to enjoy our harvest later, and not only will we benefit but so will our families overall.

Recently, my husband and I have been thinking about our future and the legacy that we want to leave behind for our children. When we decided to take a major leap of faith in August of 2018 and began laying the groundwork for The Prescription Shoppe, we had no idea what to expect. Since opening our small business in March of 2019, we have a totally new perspective on legacy.

Even when we both worked as pharmacists at a few of the big chain pharmacies, we thought about certain things like setting up a 529 account for our children and contributing to our 401(k), and we invested in life insurance. All of those decisions were responsible and would ultimately set our family up for success.

However, since becoming small-business owners and having our own personal CPA assist us in handling both our professional and personal finances, we've seen significant growth in a short time period. Now, in addition to some of the other sound decisions that we had already made on our own, we've taken things to the next level because we have someone knowledgeable advising us.

Before The Prescription Shoppe, we had dabbled a little in the stock market but not seriously. Presently, we have purchased quite a few stocks that have been successful thus far. We recently had our attorney draw up our living will and created a trust fund for our kids. Just this past April, we also decided to invest in a rental property in the Outer Banks (OBX) down in North Carolina.

Becoming small-business owners opened up a world of possibilities that we never really knew existed for us before. And if we did know about a few different opportunities here and there, we never thought we'd be in a position to take advantage of them.

This is where I'll encourage you to start thinking about how you can increase your own net worth. I recommend consulting with someone who is knowledgeable about finances and whom you trust to give you good financial advice. While I am the first to admit that I'm a pretty smart individual (we all have to toot our own horn sometimes, LOL), my specialty is pharmacy and not finances. That is why it has been beneficial for me to get counsel from someone who does specialize in finances.

Our CPA keeps us abreast of any advantages or loopholes that will specifically benefit us as small-business owners. If my husband and I continued to try and manage our own finances like we did prior to opening The Prescription Shoppe, we'd never have known how financially advantageous certain things would be for us and our business. The main takeaway here is that getting good advice is always helpful.

You also have to be willing to take a few risks. There's a saying, "Scared money don't make money!" I've learned that to be true as well. My husband and I were doing pretty well—we had phenomenal credit, we were homeowners, and we had savings in addition to our 401(k). Our lifestyle was very comfortable, and we were living the middle-class "American Dream," so to speak.

I believe that we would have continued to be fine financially and ultimately would have built up our retirement by the time we reached that stage in life. However, now we are making power moves to set up not only ourselves but our children and grandchildren.

Unfortunately, people of color are usually playing catch-up in the wealth department. Because of the history of this country, whether we are talking about slavery, reconstruction, or happenings like the Tulsa, Oklahoma, massacre on Black Wall Street—systematic racism continues to put Black and Brown people at a disadvantage. In most cases, people of color have not truly been able to build generational wealth for their families. This is a barrier that Henry and I constantly talk about and are consistently trying to make conscious decisions to overcome.

We are not financial gurus as I mentioned before. But we aren't doing too badly for ourselves, considering all that we've accomplished together by the age of thirty-five. Honestly, we still have a long way to go, and we realize that nothing is ever promised or guaranteed about our future. The goal is to continue to do the work and welcome advisement from our financial planner so that we can eventually build true generational wealth for our family.

Once you start making your own power moves and setting your family up for financial success, make sure you share your insight with your kids.

My father, Jerry Ebron, does not play about with his finances. He was always conscious about making sound financial decisions for our family. He made sure to educate my sister and me about wise ways to spend our money and foolish ways that would result in wasting our money. He constantly talked to us about how making poor financial decisions during our adolescent years could affect our lives well into adulthood. My dad impressed upon us the importance of having good credit. He ingrained in our minds that we should never, under any circumstances, cosign for anyone else. He also stressed the importance of not sharing our bank account information with anyone outside of our husbands and only after we were officially married. I know that in this day and age that advice may sound dated to some—I respect it. My dad gave us advice that he felt would benefit us as we got older. Everyone will not share the same opinions when it comes to finances. Ultimately, you have to teach your kids whatever you believe will set them up for financial success. Regardless of the advice you choose to give your children regarding money, be sure to include them in the conversation as often as possible.

I think too often parents believe that they should not include their children in discussions about their family's finances because they think, "That's grown folks' business!" Of course, I'm not encouraging you to tell your kids everything that may go on in your bank account. However, I believe that if we are going to truly build generational wealth, we have to do so by incorporating our children and future generations.

The bottom line is that no matter how financially savvy you may be and how much wealth you may build for your family, if you don't teach your kids to be good stewards of their money, they won't be able to build on the wealth that you leave for them. We've all seen stories where kids piss away their inheritance on frivolous things. That's why it's not good enough to just create wealth for them but we have to teach them how to then manage it for themselves.

My father was always big on teaching us financial steward-ship. He made sure that we had everything that we needed and most things that we wanted. However, he never gave us everything, even when he could afford to.

At the time, I didn't understand some of his lessons and thought they were merely my dad's antics. He went through this stretch where we had to open one Christmas gift per hour. In the meantime, we read the Sunday-school lesson to practice our reading comprehension.

I'm sure we were the only kids in our neighborhood who were still opening Christmas gifts up at 4:00 p.m. My sister and I would be so annoyed and thought my dad was being completely over the top. He would tell us that he was tired of watching kids rip through Christmas gifts and not fully appreciate the hard work that went into purchasing them. He wanted us to take the time to appreciate each gift before moving on to the next one. Then, I wasn't amused. Now, I fully understand what he was trying to show us. My dad didn't want my sister and me to take for granted the fact that we were privileged. He wanted us to be gracious and appreciate our blessings. Some will think his methods were a bit extreme and maybe they were. However, I can tell you that I'm one of the most gracious people you will ever meet. That's not me bragging about myself by any means—it's me expressing that no matter how outlandish I may have felt some of my dad's behavior was in my childhood, it worked!

Most things that my father taught me regarding money I agree with and will pass down to my boys. However, there is one area that we both acknowledge was a missed opportunity then.

My dad never paid my sister and me any allowance. He said the fact that we lived in his house and didn't pay any bills while he provided all of our needs was allowance enough. While I understand exactly where he was coming from now that I am a parent myself, I do intend on paying Jacob and Joshua an allowance once they get a little older.

The importance of giving your children an allowance should not be taken lightly. By giving our kids the opportunity to budget and save up for things they may want or activities that they would like to participate in can be super beneficial for them. Receiving an allowance can help your children develop discipline and restraint. If we give them the tools to succeed, they may not make some of the same financial mistakes that previous generations have made. So take the time to talk to your kids about managing their money and the value of a savings account.

When we instill in our youth an appreciation for financial stewardship, we are in turn laying the groundwork for generational wealth for our families for years to come.

➢ Create your own legacy

When we think about creating a legacy, what does that even really mean? Most of us are so focused on the here and now. Sure we may make plans here and there, and maybe we even talk about five or ten years down the line. But how many of us are thinking fifty or a hundred years down the line? And how many of us even care to think that far out?

I know that so much has occurred over the course of this past year, and most of us are just thinking about making it to the next day. While I totally get that, I still encourage you to plan right now for what you want your legacy to be later. And I'm talking about more than just the financial legacy you will leave to your children or loved ones. When you are long gone, what story do you want your children and grandchildren to tell their children? What do you want your friends and people to say about you?

My maternal grandmother, Carrie Hill, turned ninety-seven years old on July 17, 2021. Every time I think about her life, all that she's accomplished, and everyone she has loved and cared for, it makes me aspire to be like her. My grandmother has left each of her children, grandchildren, great-grandchildren, and others such a rich legacy.

She was born in North Carolina in 1924. While she was never enslaved, she was only a generation or so removed from slavery. Regardless, she still experienced oppression and racism throughout her life.

By the time she married my grandfather, George Hill, in 1942 at the age of eighteen, she was already on her way to achieving a life that most Blacks and people of color would never dream of in that day and age.

When my grandfather made his way back from World War II as an army veteran, my grandmother moved to Virginia (where my grandfather was born). They acquired one hundred acres of land by asking a white man to purchase the land on their behalf, pretending that his name was George Hill. They knew that it was unlikely that the owner would sell the land to a young, Black couple, but they figured out a way to purchase the land regardless with the help of an ally.

They then built their house on that property and began farming the land. Most people of color during that time period did not own that type of land, yet my grandparents had cleverly pulled it off. They went on to have seven children who helped them work the land when they were not in school.

And although my grandmother herself only completed grade school, she made sure that all four of "her girls" went off to college. When I think about the foundation that she laid for her family, I only hope to play the same integral role for my own family and future generations.

My mother, Janet Ebron, followed my grandmother by teaching my sister and me what it means to be a "Proverbs 31 type of woman." If you have never read Proverbs 31, take some time to check it out when you get a moment. I refer to Proverbs often for wisdom and insight, and you may find something there that you feel very strongly about as well.

My mother has led by example and has loved and supported Jasmine and me through so many things. Even now in my adult life, my mother continues to show up for me time and time again. She retired in Williamsburg, Virginia, where we live, to help my husband and me raise our two boys. Henry and I are forever indebted to her—without her, we would never have been able to accomplish everything that we have up until this point in our lives.

So when I think about my own legacy, it's something that I take extremely seriously. I want to be mindful that everything I do and say now could not only impact my future but also my future generations.

I know that thinking this far into the future may not be for everyone, but if there is any part of you that is reading this section and nodding along, I encourage you to take active steps to prepare your family for life past you and just your generation.

➢ Be sure to leave the blueprint

As you continue to grow and evolve, you will undoubtedly learn tips and life lessons along the way. You don't have to be a senior citizen to have gained some knowledge and wisdom. So as you learn and improve, don't be stingy—share your pearls of wisdom with others who could benefit. Whether a friend, family member, or someone whom you mentor, when you gain insight, you should spread the wealth! I try to do this myself in multiple ways, both in my career and personal life.

Not only do I have the opportunity to precept Hampton University School of Pharmacy students because The Prescription Shoppe is a preceptor site (we won the 2020 Experiential Site of the Year Award) but I also become a mentor to my students. In most cases, a lot of the students that come on their five-week rotations with us have never seen a Black-owned, independent pharmacy—let alone worked in one. Because my husband and I realize that representation matters, we use these rotations as a way to encourage, support, and inspire our students. Oftentimes, we are not that much older than them, but we still can provide them with guidance.

As Hampton University School of Pharmacy alumni ourselves, we can relate to their experiences of attending a Historically Black College and University (HBCU); there's absolutely nothing like it. The sense of community and acceptance that you feel while you're attending an HBCU is priceless, but it also comes with challenges. The resources are not usually on the same level as those at predominantly white universities, and this is even more of an issue at a private institution like Hampton.

Regardless, you figure it out, you do what needs to be done to graduate, and your experiences build character and a certain grit. Plus, you make lifelong bonds with people who you consider more your family than just your friends.

When we interact with our rotation students, we become a resource for them in more ways than one. In addition to teaching them how an independent pharmacy runs and showing them the impact that we have on the daily lives of our patients as community pharmacists, we also discuss life post-graduation.

Our students value our opinions and feedback, and they stay in contact with us after they graduate. Some of them ask for recommendation letters, and others ask for personal advice. All in all, it is super fulfilling to know that I am having a positive influence on the many students that walk through our doors.

I also mentor young ladies from sixth to twelfth grade in the Ladies of Virtue and Elegance (L. O. V. E.) Ministry at my church, New Zion Baptist Church. This particular ministry focuses on helping young women plan for their futures by offering career days so that they can hear from different types of professionals who look like them, organizing community service projects to teach them the importance of investing in their own communities, and arranging college tours so that they can start taking steps to prepare for life after their high school graduation. Giving back to the youth by spending time with them is just as much of a win for me as it is for them.

Honestly, I don't really know if any of the young adults that I interact with will remember me twenty years down the line. They may forget my name and maybe even my face, but my hope is that something that I have said or done will leave a lasting impression on them.

I say all of this to emphasize, leave a blueprint behind. Find ways to assist and inspire others along your journey. If you are doing well, great for you! Ultimately, you're really winning when you spread the wealth around.

Faith over Fear

When people hear the word "faith," a few definitions may come to mind. Google says faith is the "complete trust or confidence in someone or something." You will also see mention of "a system of religious beliefs." And while the Bible mentions the word faith repeatedly, one of the best definitions in my opinion can be found in Hebrews 11:1; it reads: "Now faith is the assurance of things hoped for, the conviction of things not seen." In a nutshell, you have faith that something will happen without having any proof or confirmation ahead of time.

Regardless of whether you are a spiritual person or not, we have all been hopeful for something at some point in our lives. Each of us has experienced moments where we may have prayed or wished for a circumstance to turn around on our behalf. Whether you realize it or not, faith impacts every area of our life. When we go to sleep at night, we trust that we will wake up the next morning. When we leave our homes, we expect to return safely. The bottom line is that faith keeps us going.

➢ The faith of a mustard seed

For some, the mustard seed signifies good luck. However, in Christianity, the mustard seed is a symbol of faith. The Bible tells us that we only need the faith of a mustard seed to move mountains—God rewards us for trusting Him. The word "faith" is mentioned countless times in the Bible, and there are numerous examples of people who were faithful in the midst of uncertain circumstances. Ultimately, each and every one of us will have doubts and experience worry at some point over the course of our lives. How we choose to deal with it is up to us!

Faith has kept me grounded more times than I can count over the course of my thirty-four years on this planet. My best friend died from leukemia when I was fourteen years old. Kara and I had been best friends since kindergarten. She got diagnosed on February 21 and died on September 28 of that same year. It was my first experience with death that I can remember, to the point where I couldn't fully process the fact that she was actually gone. I remember being shocked and devastated all at once.

Because my parents had instilled such a sense of faith in both my sister and me at a young age, I was able to cope. Doesn't mean it doesn't still affect me—I still cry on her birthday or the day she passed almost every year. I always wonder who she would be if she was still here or how her life would have impacted my own.

But my faith continues to get me through and reminds me that everything works out according to God's plan.

As I mentioned before, my mother is a two-time cancer survivor, and now so is my forty-year-old sister. Dealing with cancer is never fun, and to say that the journey is tough would be a huge understatement. But ultimately my faith sustained me and my family through those journeys as well.

Even getting through pharmacy school required a level of faith, and without it I wouldn't be Dr. Jade L. Ranger today. There has not been a single season in my life that faith has not played an active role.

So again, I encourage you to tap into your spirituality and allow yourself to feel the presence of a higher power and something bigger than yourself. Having a relationship with God has never meant that I don't experience trials or tribulations. I've had my fair share of ups and downs, but all the while, my faith has seen me through.

I can't imagine the deep ends that I would have gone off of if I had to go at life alone. Do I have a loving family and friends who I depend on? Of course! But some of life's dark moments are so dark that only the love of Christ can illuminate them. I know that He will never leave or forsake me. I know that I can count on the love and comfort that only Jesus can provide. And ultimately I know that everyone else whom I love is only human.

Your friends, family, and even significant others will eventually let you down; they will disappoint you and maybe even hurt you to your core. When this occurs (and at some point, it will), if you have a relationship with Christ, I have learned that it is His strength that will sustain you and bring you through—whatever circumstances you may be facing either publicly or privately even right now in this moment.

Whether you are dealing with a marriage on the rocks, a crossroads in your career, or just searching for contentment, spirituality can keep you encouraged and help you to discern which way you should go. And while I won't start preaching to you and give you a full-blown sermon, I hope that you will take some time to evaluate where you are in your spiritual walk today and make adjustments accordingly.

➤ Stay connected

Having a relationship with God is ongoing. You can't just express your love for Christ once and then keep on moving with your daily life. Being in accord with the Lord means constantly communing with Him. Too often people think that in order to be a Christian, you have to walk around praying all day or being perfect.

Then there are those who have tried to use Christ as a scapegoat and claim that He is the reason why they believe so strongly in certain things. There's also the group of folks who believe that all religions are hypocritical and unauthentic.

I can't speak for anyone else but myself, and to me, my faith is very real.

By taking the time to talk with God daily about my wins and losses, I feel more connected to Him because I include Him. Before I make a decision, big or small, I consult with God through prayer. Sometimes I talk to Him when I'm driving, in the shower, out for a run, or even in Target. There's never a time where I feel that God doesn't hear me or is unavailable.

Staying connected to God has not only helped me to overcome past life experiences that could have derailed me but His love continues to help me get through my day-to-day routine. Faith isn't just for when your world is turned upside down— your faith can lead you through the good times as well.

Oftentimes, I become overwhelmed by my blessings. While I'm thankful for my family and the success of our small business, I'd be lying if I said that my responsibilities haven't taken a toll on me.

I'm sure many of you know what it's like for things in your life to be going well but still feeling insanely depressed or anxious. I can't say that I have ever suffered from depression, but I do believe that anxiety comes along with my obsessive-compulsive disorder (OCD). I tend to be paranoid and at times feel like I don't deserve all of my blessings. I'll then feel fearful that a shoe is getting ready to drop somewhere that will ruin everything. I'll worry about my husband and kids or my parents or be convinced that something at The Prescription

Shoppe is going to go wrong. And who knows, maybe this is just regular human behavior and has absolutely nothing to do with my OCD (like a lot of people, I tend to self-diagnose my own ailments). Regardless, reading scripture and doing my daily devotional reminds me of God's love and His faithfulness.

So I hope you will choose to stay connected spiritually also in whatever form that looks like for you. Whether through prayer, meditation, or anything else that reminds you that the world is bigger than you and your problems. Staying connected can provide you with the willpower to overcome the trials of life and help you thrive in the midst of any circumstance.

My faith keeps me grounded, and it also keeps me motivated. Ultimately, I know that what God has ordained for me will be for me, which is why I keep pushing forward and allow myself to dream bigger every step of the way.

➤ Don't let fear stop you from accomplishing your goals

Too often, we have a desire to pursue an idea or a passion of ours, but we let fear stand in our way. Fear of failure, fear of embarrassment, fear of rejection, and the list goes on. But ask yourself if what you fear most is the worst-case scenario? Do you think that if you try and fail, you would be unable to make a comeback? Is being embarrassed really that bad if you at least took your shot? And if you get rejected the first time, does that mean that you stop trying?

If the success of The Prescription Shoppe has taught me nothing else, it's taught me to dream big and keep it going. When my husband came to me in July of 2018 asking me to seriously consider opening our own pharmacy, I literally cringed to myself. Henry had brought this topic up before somewhat jokingly over the years, but this time I could tell that he was dead serious.

I'm not a big risk taker, y'all! I tend to be calculated and measured—always erring on the side of caution. At the time, I felt that things were going well and there was no need to rock the boat. I didn't see the need to turn our lives upside down to chase a dream that was not guaranteed.

We were living a comfortable lifestyle, our careers were consistent, and we had a young family as I mentioned before. Henry's career had really taken off as a pharmacy clinical services manager with Walmart, and no one would have expected him to just quit. In fact, most of his colleagues thought that he would continue to climb the corporate ladder. But my husband is an ambitious one, and he felt that no matter how well his career was going, he no longer felt fulfilled in his current role and wanted to make a change.

Talk about the faith of a mustard seed—it took all of the faith I could muster up in order for me to agree to take this entrepreneurial journey with him. Our original plan was that I would continue to work part time with Walmart for the first year and a half until we saw how things with The Prescription Shoppe were going to pan out.

Our grand opening was on March 6, 2019. By June of 2019, I felt like I could literally hear the Holy Spirit telling me that I wasn't fully trusting that God would provide all of our needs. The reoccurring thought was that while I had taken a leap of faith to an extent, I was still holding on to my safety net (which was my job with Walmart). I felt that I was being led to quit and go all in with The Prescription Shoppe. It was like God was telling me, "If you fully trust me, I will take this endeavor beyond your wildest dreams!" Of course, I was stubborn and kept holding out. Even though friends and family members kept encouraging me to quit, I just couldn't fathom not having a backup plan.

My husband and I had some pretty contentious conversations over the course of the summer of 2019. Henry also believed that I should leave Walmart and help him run things full time at our store. If I'm being honest, I was scared that I would quit my job, things would fall apart, and Henry and I would both be out of work.

Now, in our field it's not like we would have been unable to find employment if things did eventually go south, but at the time I was working only eight minutes down the road from our house, and I didn't want to lose my position there and then not be able to get it back.

Fear is so real—it can paralyze you and prevent you from pursuing better opportunities. Not knowing that things will work out and that you will become "successful" has stopped a lot of people dead in their tracks—it almost stopped me also.

I want you to know that no matter how scared you may be to pursue your dream(s), the fear of being complacent and unfulfilled should freak you out even more.

There are so many people who are not happy and continue to do the same thing day in and day out. They go to a job that they hate, or they stay in a relationship in which they are undervalued and underserved, and they are totally miserable.

Who wants to live like that indefinitely? Again, no one has a perfect life, job, or relationship—all of these will take time and energy to make them work.

However, if you are happy and fully invested, you will feel more inclined to push through the bad times because you know that you have way more good ones. So take the leap of faith off the edge that you have been teetering on for weeks, months, or even years. The freedom that you feel will be so worth it and make your life that much more worthwhile.

➢ Along with your God-given purpose comes His provision

I am sure that I am not the only one who second-guesses myself or wonders if I have made the right decisions from time to time. Whenever I get a bright idea, the very next thing I do is start questioning myself. I feel nervous or a little anxious about whether or not my idea will work or actually be successful. Even when I am mulling over something that has nothing to do with my career, I tend to obsess over making the right choices and can stress myself out. If you can relate and have ever found yourself wondering if you are on the right path or if you made a wrong turn, this section is for you!

God does not want us to waste our talents. When He gives us a desire to do something, He will provide a way, but there's one caveat—we have to trust Him fully.

Finally, on October 22, 2019, I put in my two-week notice with my job. Although I did not have a clue what would happen next, the calm that I experienced after I sent that email was supernatural. I physically felt a weight lifted off of my chest, and it was the freest I had ever felt in my life. It was like God said, "Okay cool, you decided to trust me; now let's go get it!"

It's funny because at first I questioned whether or not I was hearing the Holy Spirit leading me to leave Walmart or if I was talking myself into quitting because I was over it. I kept thinking that I would quit and then God would be like, "I never told you to do that." But once that weight was removed from my spirit, I knew instantly that I was making a decision in line with God's will for my life. Just as He promised, things really took off with our small business once I decided to come aboard full time. And while we are still a young business, the journey has been almost unbelievable thus far.

The way that God set up so many opportunities on our behalf and allowed us to make countless connections has been awesome to watch. In addition to numerous awards and accolades, board of directors' appointments, and public-speaking engagements, we have been able to impact our community in more ways than one.

The other thing that I find to be amazing is that through The Prescription Shoppe, God has allowed me to tap into so many of my talents and gifts that were sitting dormant before. Whether being a contributor to our local newspaper, *The Virginia Gazette*, writing blog posts for our website, or even writing this book—my love of reading and writing has come full circle. I never thought I would be using my writing skills in my profession, but as it turns out the Lord had other plans.

I've also been able to use my voice in ways that I would have never expected. Because of The Prescription Shoppe, I have a platform within the Greater Williamsburg community and have been able to raise social justice awareness in ways that I probably would not have been able to if I had never put in my resignation with my previous job.

God has also given me the opportunity to learn new things and grow in areas that I would have never guessed. I told y'all that I was so not a social media person prior to becoming a small-business owner, I actually avoided it like the plague. But now I find joy in managing all of our social-media sites and engaging with our followers. Did it take me some time to get the hang of it? Yes. Am I still figuring things out as I go? Absolutely! However, the bottom line is that I'm having a positive impact, and I'm thankful for this opportunity.

I know that I've talked a lot about my own personal experiences. I'm hopeful that you all will see through my journey how faith can be your determining factor as well—whether you believe in a higher power and/or yourself, faith is the key!

The moral of the story is not to limit yourself by letting fear get in the way of your dreams. The other major takeaway is that if God gives you a vision, He will certainly bless you with His provision.

Will everything be perfect and go smoothly all of the time? Probably not. Chances are you will have struggles and challenges and obstacles that will try to get in your way; don't let anything stop you from becoming the phenomenal woman and person that God has already ordained for you to be. Trust Him with your hopes and dreams. Let Him order your steps and guide your plans. Be open to His feedback and make adjustments accordingly. Most importantly, never stop dreaming bigger dreams and then chasing them with all of your might. Don't forget to tap into what I like to call your "mustard seed mentality" along the way!

Acknowledgments

I want to thank God—first, for giving me the vision to write this book and second, for granting me the faith of a mustard seed in order to complete it.

Next, I'd like to thank my loving husband and best friend, Henry, for supporting me in all of my dreams and endeavors. When I first told him that I wanted to write a book because I love to write and thought that my life lessons and experiences could be helpful and empower other women in various walks of life, he immediately told me, "Go for it!" Without hesitation, he would listen as I would read him different sections of my manuscript after having a long day himself. Henry gave me honest feedback and allowed me to bounce ideas off of him. He wouldn't interrupt me when he knew I was up late again writing (I basically typed this entire book on my phone, LOL). When I doubted myself and my ability, he cheered me on. Most of all, he held this secret for me for several months and honored my wishes to keep my aspirations of becoming an author between us (partially because I wasn't sure if I'd ever actually finish this book and partially because I was too nervous to admit that I was even trying).

Then there is Hannah Sheinkman, my writing coach. I told her my vision and the message that I wanted to get across but admitted that I was overwhelmed thinking about when I would have time to actually write a whole book. She gave me the best advice—just write whatever comes to your mind and heart for thirty minutes a day. So that's what I did; here and there, whenever I had a little time at the end of an evening or while I was waiting for a dentist appointment, I'd add another entry. Hannah's feedback and constructive criticism was always positive and helpful. And while she couldn't relate to all of my life experiences personally, she helped me grow and mature as a writer—I'll forever be grateful.

To my parents, Jerry and Janet Ebron, thank you for your constant love and support. You taught me to love God, myself, and others and showed me how to be gracious yet confident. I'll spend the rest of my life trying to set the example for my boys that you did for Jasmine and me. Thanks for everything you showed me about life when you thought I wasn't looking.

Jasmine, you have been a role model, big sister, best friend, and confidant all in one. Thanks for always giving me affirmations and reminding me that I can do anything that I set my mind to.

A *major* thank you to all of my family and friends for keeping me grounded and always having my back. I appreciate anyone who has ever given me advice or poured into me along my journey.

Last but not least, thank you to my children, Jacob and Joshua. I love you two more than all of the words in all of the languages in all the world—meaning, beyond measure. You have made me a better person and taught me so much about myself. Mommy is so proud of the little young men you are becoming. Stay humble, treat others the way you want to be treated, and always believe in yourselves.

And if I may add one more thank you...to everyone who took the time to read through these pages, whether in its entirety or just a few chapters, I appreciate you. Thank you for your time and attention; I hope you found a pearl or two of wisdom that may have been helpful in your own lives.

CPSIA information can be obtained
at www.ICGtesting.com
Printed in the USA
BVHW091013141121
621604BV00013B/1085